EP
Geography and Cultures
Printables:
Levels 5-8

This book belongs to:

_____

This book was made for your convenience. It is available for printing from the Easy Peasy All-in-One Homeschool website. It contains all of the printables from Easy Peasy's geography and cultures course. The instructions for each page are found in the online course.

Easy Peasy All-in-One Homeschool is a free online homeschool curriculum providing high quality education for children around the globe. It provides complete courses for preschool through high school graduation. For EP's curriculum visit allinonehomeschool.com.

EP Geography and Cultures Printables: Levels 5-8

ISBN: 9798566574752

First Edition: December 2020

Latitude and Longitude

Use the map to fill in the blanks below. Which location or Chinese province would you find at the coordinates given?

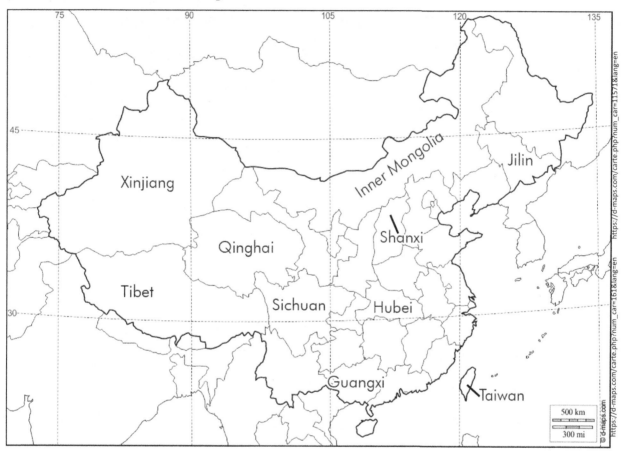

27° latitude, 122° longitude _____

45° latitude, 90° longitude _____

32° latitude, 100° longitude _____

43° latitude, 125° longitude _____

37° latitude, 112° longitude _____

World Map

Passport

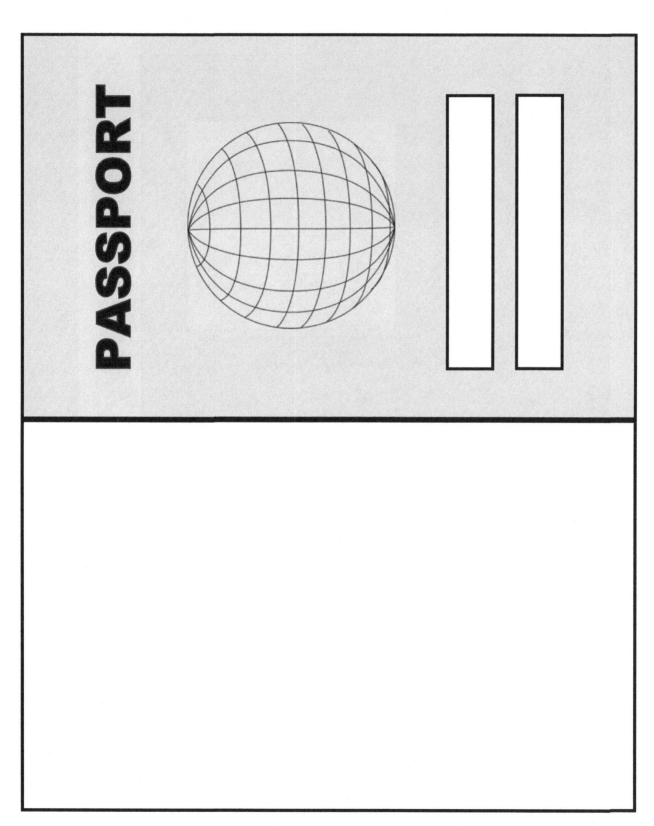

(This page left intentionally blank)

Country: _____

Picture of flag:

Name: _____

Nationality: _____

Gender: _____

Date of birth: _____

Date of issue: _____

Date of expiration: _____

Picture

Signature: _____

(This page left intentionally blank)

Countries visited:

Countries visited:

(This page left intentionally blank)

Countries visited:

Countries visited:

(This page left intentionally blank)

United Kingdom

Using the map linked online, label each country of the UK on this map: England, Wales, Scotland, and Northern Ireland. Color each country a different color. Label each capital: London, England; Cardiff, Wales; Edinburgh, Scotland; Belfast, Northern Ireland.

History of England

History:	Flag:
_____ _____ _____ _____ _____ _____ _____	

Population	
Languages	
Religions	
Government	
Industries/Resources	
Exports	

Map:

World Map

3000 km (equat.)

2000 mi (equat.)

© d-maps.com

https://d-maps.com/m/world/centreeurope/centreeurope22.gif

France

Using the map linked online, label the map of France following the directions below.

Label France's capital, Paris.

Label Mount Blanc, France's highest point.

Label the path of the Pyrenees Mountains and the Alps.

Label the Bay of Biscay.

Label the Seine and Loire Rivers.

History of France

History:

_____

_____

_____

_____

_____

_____

Flag:

Population	
Languages	
Religions	
Government	
Industries/Resources	
Exports	

Map:

Europe

Label what you can of this map. You can simply point and verbally name the countries if you'd like. Do you remember any capitals?

South Africa

Using the map linked online, label the map following the directions below.

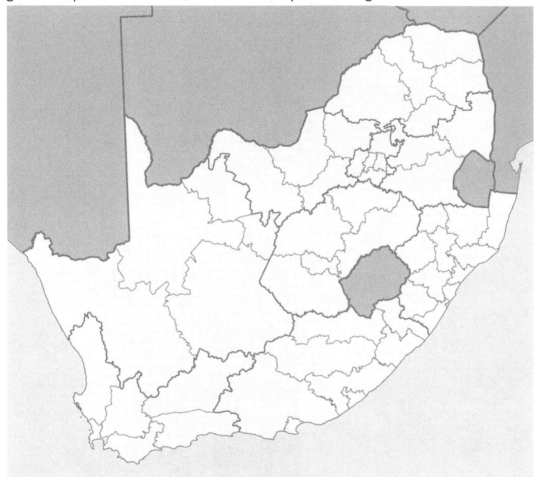

Label South Africa's administrative capital, Pretoria.

Label South Africa's judiciary capital, Bloemfontein.

Label South Africa's legislative capital, Cape Town.

Label the Indian Ocean.

Label the Atlantic Ocean.

Africa

Follow the directions in the online course to label the map.

South African Flag

Color the South African flag. There's an image linked in the online course to help you.

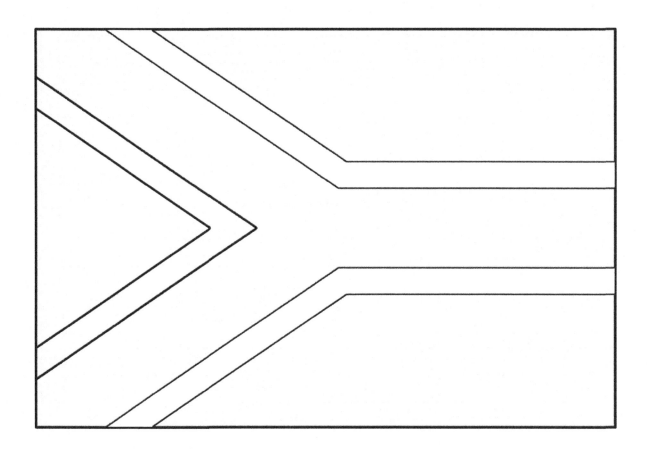

South Africa

History:

_____
_____
_____
_____
_____
_____
_____

Nelson Mandela

_____
_____
_____
_____
_____
_____
_____

Population	
Languages	
Religions	
Government	
Industries/Resources	
Exports	

Kenya

Using the map linked online, label the map of Kenya following the directions below.

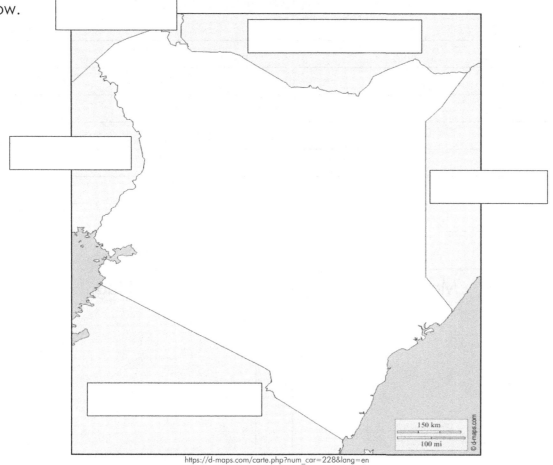

https://d-maps.com/carte.php?num_car=228&lang=en

Label Kenya's capital, Nairobi.

Label the surrounding countries of Ethiopia, Tanzania, Uganda, Somalia, and South Sudan.

Label Lake Victoria and the Indian Ocean.

Label these mountains: Mt. Elgon, Mt. Kenya, and Mt. Kulal.

Label the Tana and Athi Rivers.

Kenya

History:

_____

_____

_____

_____

_____

_____

_____

Map:

Flag:

Population	
Languages	
Religions	
Government	
Industries/Resources	
Exports	

Nigeria

Label the map of Nigeria following the directions below.

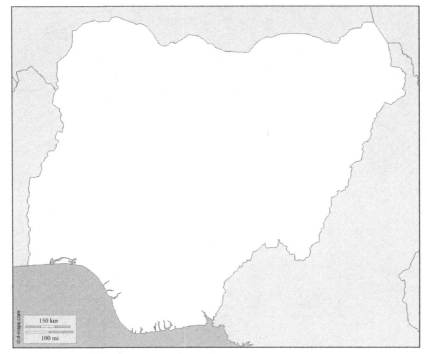

https://d-maps.com/carte.php?num_car=1206&lang=en

Label Nigeria's capital, Abuja.

Label Nigeria's former capital, Lagos.

Label the path of the Niger River.

Label the surrounding countries of Benin, Niger, Chad, and Cameroon.

Label the Gulf of Guinea.

Australia

Label the map of Australia following the directions below.

Label Australia's capital, Canberra.

Label the city of Sydney.

Label Kangaroo Island.

Label the following: Indian Ocean, Pacific Ocean, Southern Ocean.

Label the Great Barrier Reef.

Eastern Hemisphere

Use the online directions to label your map.

Asia

Use this map as you begin to learn the countries of Asia in the online course.
Show which countries were not included in your lesson.

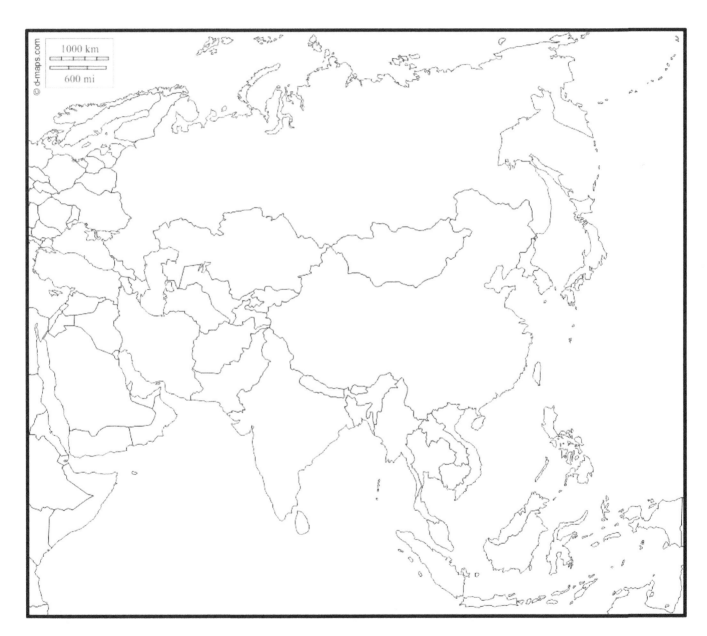

https://d-maps.com/carte.php?num_car=55&lang=en

India

Label this map of India using the directions below.

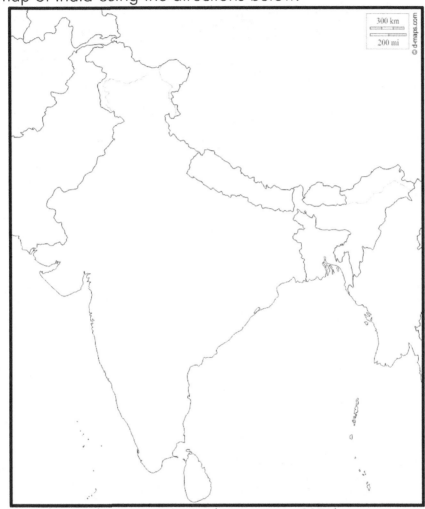

https://d-maps.com/carte.php?num_car=287&lang=en

Label India's capital, New Dehli.

Label the Bay of Bengal.

Label the Arabian Sea.

Label the following countries: India, Pakistan, Afghanistan, Tajikistan, China, Nepal, Bhutan, Bangladesh, and Myanmar.

Label Sri Lanka.

History of India

History:

_____

_____

_____

_____

_____

_____

_____

Map:

Flag:

Population	
Languages	
Religions	
Government	
Industries/Resources	
Exports	

India

Answer the following questions to discover the hidden treasure. Once you have all the answers, follow the instructions at the bottom of the page to see if you found the treasure!

1. The _____ Caves are thirty-four monasteries and temples cut into the cliffs.

___ ___ ___ ___ ___ ___

2. This country is the only country where Hinduism is the official religion.

___ ___ ___ ___ ___

3. In India's caste system, people are born into groups, or _____, each with a different status in society.

___ ___ ___ ___ ___ ___

4. The game Chaturanga is thought to be the origin of the game of _____.

___ ___ ___ ___ ___

5. What vegetable is used in the Indian sweet gajar ka halwa?

___ ___ ___ ___ ___ ___

Now that you have all your answers, write the first letter from each answer in order on the blank below (no spaces or punctuation, just the lower case letters):

allinonehomeschool.com/_____

Enter this address in your browser to see if you got all the questions correct and found the treasure. (If you get an error message, check your answers again!)

Japan

Label this map of Japan using the directions below.

https://d-maps.com/carte.php?num_car=360&lang=en

Label Japan's capital, Tokyo.

Label the city of Hiroshima. What happened there?

Label Japan's four islands: Hokkaido, Honshu, Kyushu, Shikoku.

Label the Sea of Japan.

Label the Pacific Ocean.

History of Russia

History:

_____
_____
_____
_____
_____
_____
_____

Map:

Flag:

Population	
Languages	
Religions	
Government	
Industries/Resources	
Exports	

(This page left intentionally blank)

Antarctic Expedition

Cut the pages on the dotted lines and place them in this pattern: $\begin{smallmatrix}1&2\\3&4\end{smallmatrix}$ Using a single six-sided die and whatever markers you can gather (coins, different rocks, pawns from other games, etc.), take turns rolling and moving the number on the die. Follow the directions on the square you land on. Requested facts can be found throughout the board. Can you get to the end and complete the expedition?

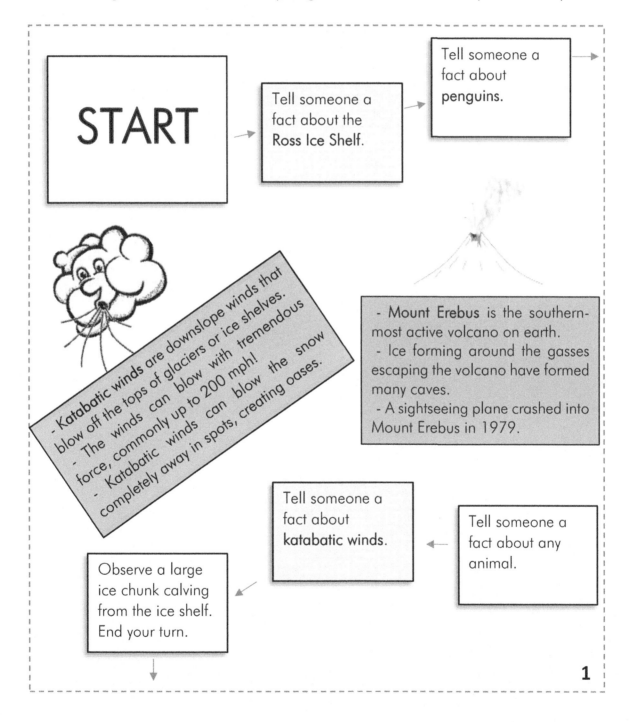

START

Tell someone a fact about the **Ross Ice Shelf.**

Tell someone a fact about **penguins.**

- Katabatic winds are downslope winds that blow off the tops of glaciers or ice shelves.
- The winds can blow with tremendous force, commonly up to 200 mph!
- Katabatic winds can blow the snow completely away in spots, creating oases.

- **Mount Erebus** is the southernmost active volcano on earth.
- Ice forming around the gasses escaping the volcano have formed many caves.
- A sightseeing plane crashed into Mount Erebus in 1979.

Tell someone a fact about **katabatic winds.**

Tell someone a fact about any animal.

Observe a large ice chunk calving from the ice shelf. End your turn.

1

(This page left intentionally blank)

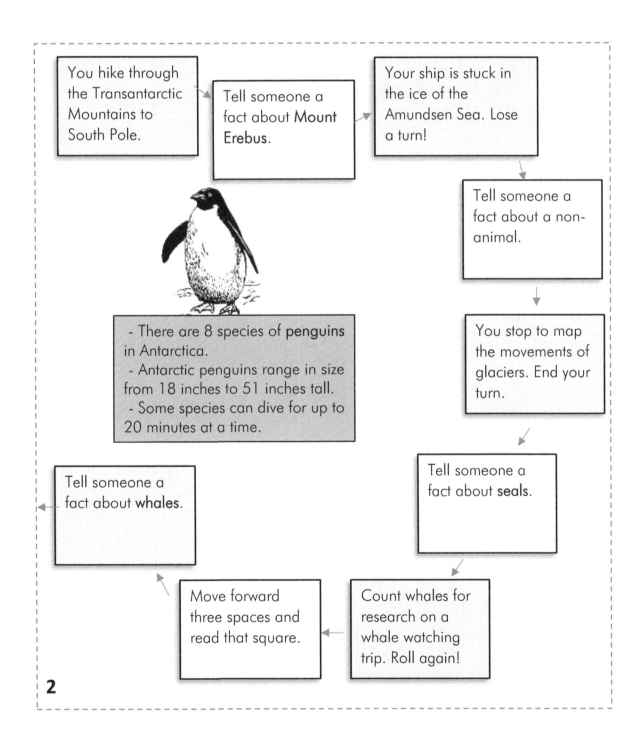

You hike through the Transantarctic Mountains to South Pole.

Tell someone a fact about **Mount Erebus**.

Your ship is stuck in the ice of the Amundsen Sea. Lose a turn!

Tell someone a fact about a non-animal.

You stop to map the movements of glaciers. End your turn.

- There are 8 species of **penguins** in Antarctica.
- Antarctic penguins range in size from 18 inches to 51 inches tall.
- Some species can dive for up to 20 minutes at a time.

Tell someone a fact about **seals**.

Tell someone a fact about **whales**.

Move forward three spaces and read that square.

Count whales for research on a whale watching trip. Roll again!

2

(This page left intentionally blank)

3

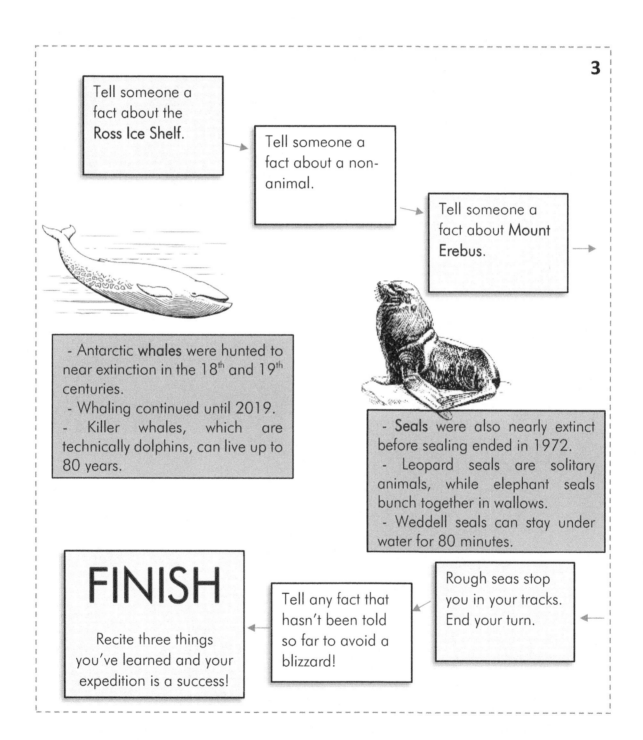

Tell someone a fact about the **Ross Ice Shelf**.

Tell someone a fact about a non-animal.

Tell someone a fact about **Mount Erebus**.

- Antarctic **whales** were hunted to near extinction in the 18th and 19th centuries.
- Whaling continued until 2019.
- Killer whales, which are technically dolphins, can live up to 80 years.

- **Seals** were also nearly extinct before sealing ended in 1972.
- Leopard seals are solitary animals, while elephant seals bunch together in wallows.
- Weddell seals can stay under water for 80 minutes.

FINISH

Recite three things you've learned and your expedition is a success!

Tell any fact that hasn't been told so far to avoid a blizzard!

Rough seas stop you in your tracks. End your turn.

(This page left intentionally blank)

4

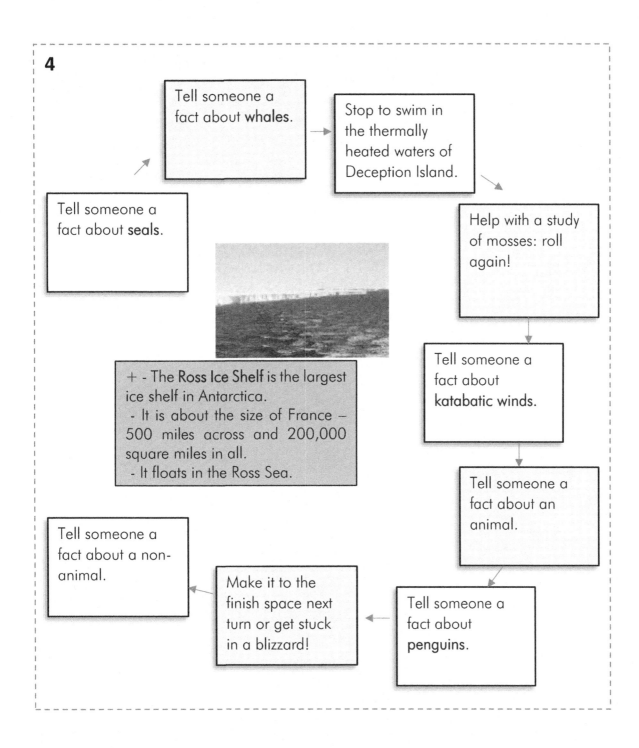

Tell someone a fact about **whales**.

Stop to swim in the thermally heated waters of Deception Island.

Tell someone a fact about **seals**.

Help with a study of mosses: roll again!

+ - The **Ross Ice Shelf** is the largest ice shelf in Antarctica.
- It is about the size of France – 500 miles across and 200,000 square miles in all.
- It floats in the Ross Sea.

Tell someone a fact about **katabatic winds**.

Tell someone a fact about an animal.

Tell someone a fact about a non-animal.

Make it to the finish space next turn or get stuck in a blizzard!

Tell someone a fact about **penguins**.

(This page left intentionally blank)

South America

Use this map of South America along with the online lessons.

History of Brazil

History:

_____

_____

_____

_____

_____

_____

Map:

Flag:

Population	
Languages	
Religions	
Government	
Industries/Resources	
Exports	

Argentina

Label this map of Argentina using the directions below.

https://d-maps.com/carte.php?num_car=1458&lang=en

Label Argentina's capital, Buenos Aires.

Label the Pacific and Atlantic oceans.

Label the surrounding countries of Chile, Bolivia, Paraguay, Brazil, and Uruguay.

Mark on the map where the Andes Mountains are.

History of Argentina

History:

_____

_____

_____

_____

_____

_____

_____

Map:

Flag:

Population	
Languages	
Religions	
Government	
Industries/Resources	
Exports	

Landforms of the World

Fill in definitions or pictures of the words. The important thing is knowing what they are.

Altitude	Archipelago	Arroyo
Badlands	Basin	Bay
Bluff	Branch (tributary)	Canal
Cliff	Delta	Estuary
Fjord	Glacier	Inlet

Landforms of the World

Fill in definitions or pictures of the words. The important thing is knowing what they are.

Island	Isthmus	Mesa
Mountain Range	Mouth (river)	Oasis
Peninsula	Plateau	Port
Reef	Reservoir	Sea
Source (river)	Strait	Terrace

Central America

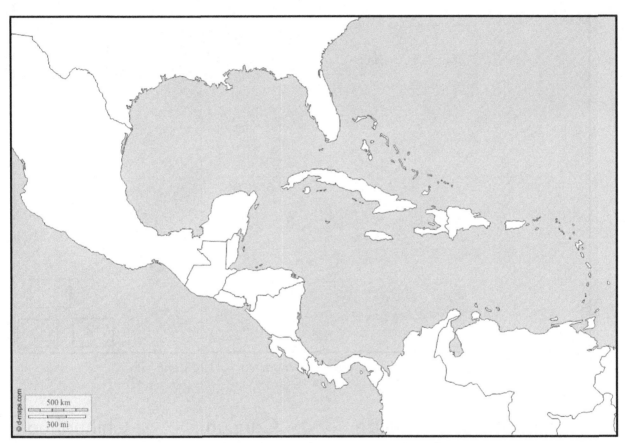

https://d-maps.com/carte.php?num_car=1388&lang=en

Mexico

Fill in the blanks below with the number from the map. The plain numbers are cities. The boxed numbers are countries.

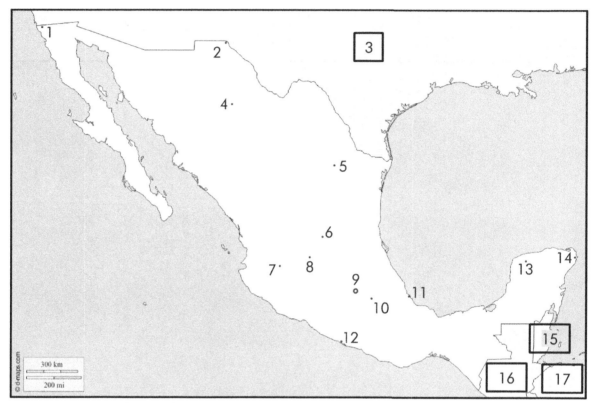

https://d-maps.com/carte.php?num_car=4124&lang=en

___Acapulco   ____Belize   ____Cancun   ____Chihuahua

____Juarez   ____Guadalajara   ____Guatemala   ____Honduras

____Leon   ____Merida   ____Mexico City   ____Monterrey

____Puebla   ____San Luis Potosi   ____Tijuana

____United States   ____Veracruz

North America

1000 km

600 mi

© d-maps.com

History of Mexico

History:

_____

_____

_____

_____

_____

_____

_____

Map:

Flag:

Population	
Languages	
Religions	
Government	
Industries/Resources	
Exports	

United States of America

Use this map to learn the postal abbreviations of the US states.

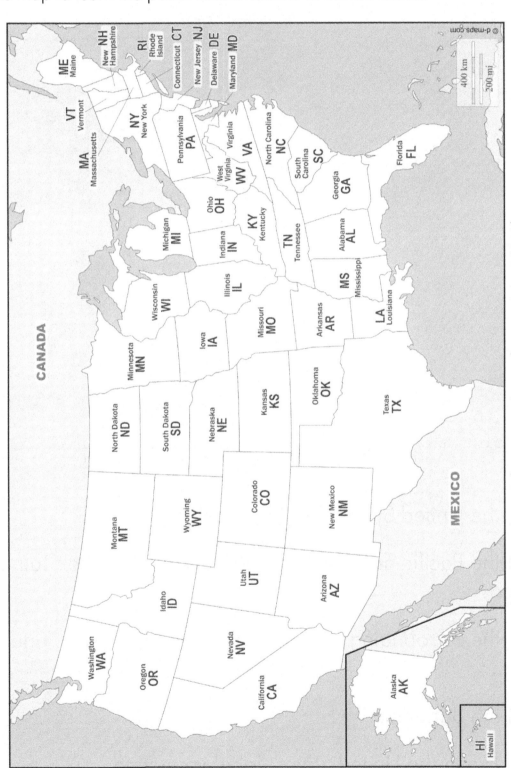

United States of America

Label this map of the United States using the directions below.

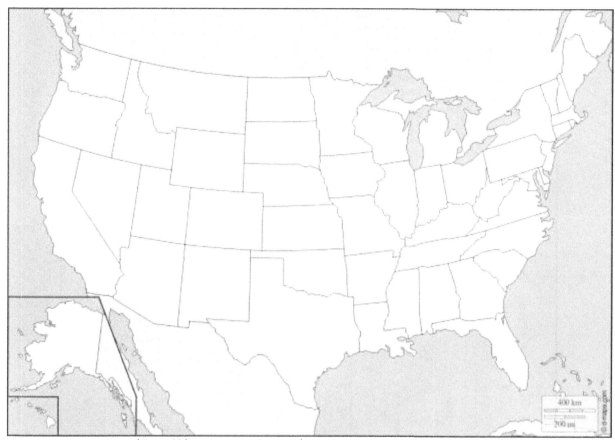

https://d-maps.com/carte.php?num_car=1652&lang=en

Label the United States' capital, Washington, D.C.

Label the Pacific and Atlantic oceans as well as the Gulf of Mexico.

Label the surrounding countries of Canada, Mexico, and Cuba.

Label the Bahamas.

If you live in the United States, label your state.

United States of America

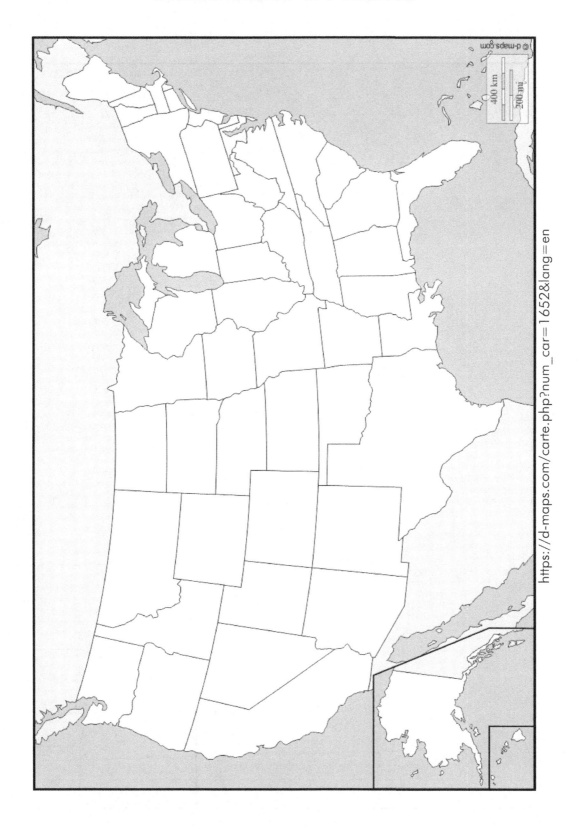

United States of America

Use this map to answer the questions on the next page.

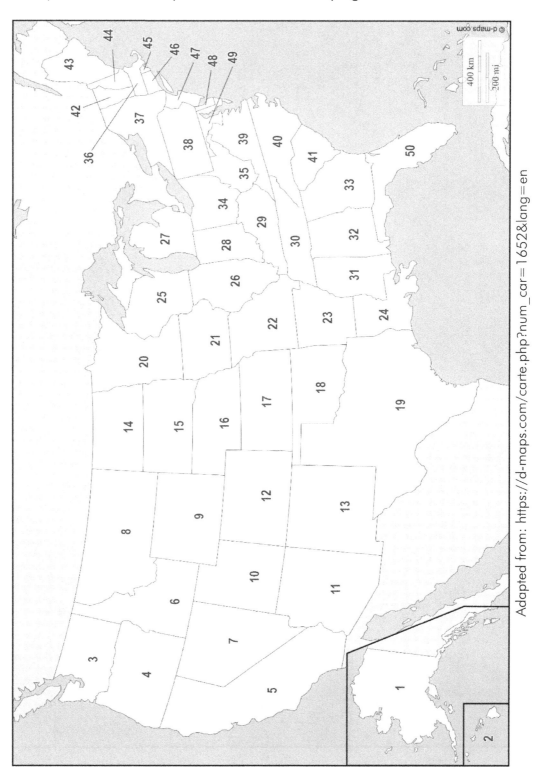

United States of America

Fill in each state's postal abbreviation, and then write its number from the map on the previous page.

_____ Alabama	_____	_____ Montana	_____
_____ Alaska	_____	_____ Nebraska	_____
_____ Arizona	_____	_____ Nevada	_____
_____ Arkansas	_____	_____ New Hampshire	_____
_____ California	_____	_____ New Jersey	_____
_____ Colorado	_____	_____ New Mexico	_____
_____ Connecticut	_____	_____ New York	_____
_____ Delaware	_____	_____ North Carolina	_____
_____ Florida	_____	_____ North Dakota	_____
_____ Georgia	_____	_____ Ohio	_____
_____ Hawaii	_____	_____ Oklahoma	_____
_____ Idaho	_____	_____ Oregon	_____
_____ Illinois	_____	_____ Pennsylvania	_____
_____ Indiana	_____	_____ Rhode Island	_____
_____ Iowa	_____	_____ South Carolina	_____
_____ Kansas	_____	_____ South Dakota	_____
_____ Kentucky	_____	_____ Tennessee	_____
_____ Louisiana	_____	_____ Texas	_____
_____ Maine	_____	_____ Utah	_____
_____ Maryland	_____	_____ Vermont	_____
_____ Massachussetts	_____	_____ Virginia	_____
_____ Michigan	_____	_____ Washington	_____
_____ Minnesota	_____	_____ West Virginia	_____
_____ Mississippi	_____	_____ Wisconsin	_____
_____ Missouri	_____	_____ Wyoming	_____

State Nicknames

Use the clues to figure out which state goes in the blank.

I'm known as the Land of the Midnight Sun.
I'm a very snowy place.
I'm not bordered by any other states.

_____

I'm known as the Sunshine State.
I'm a peninsula.
My islands are known as Keys.

_____

I'm known as the Great Lakes State.
One of the lakes divides me into separate pieces.
One of my bordering neighbors is Canada.

_____

I'm known as the Ocean State.
Hearing my name might make you think of an ocean.
I'm the smallest state.

_____

I'm known as the Show-Me State.
Some also call me the Gateway to the West.
One of my cities has a giant Gateway Arch.

_____

Made in United States
North Haven, CT
04 May 2024